Optical le

For Lida
who is going
to be my slave
for a while.
Little did she
know!
David K

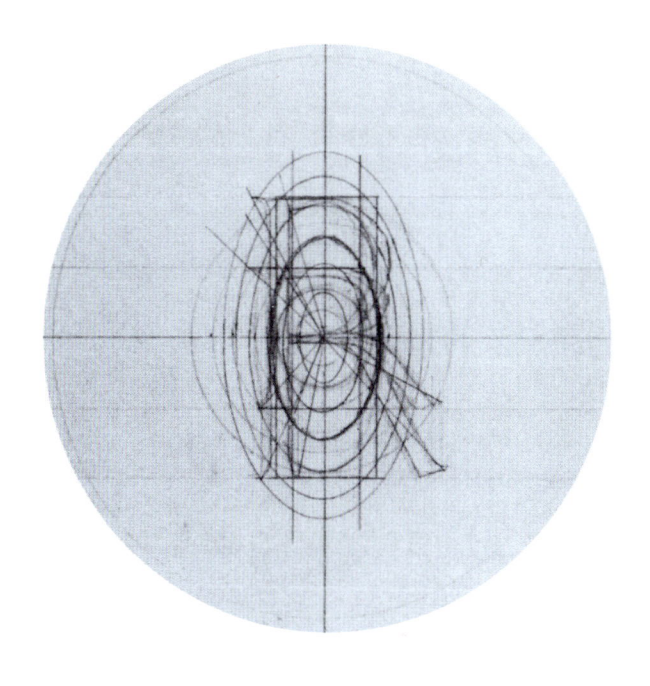

Optical letter spacing

FOR NEW PRINTING SYSTEMS

David Kindersley

EDITED BY
Lida Lopes Cardozo Kindersley

CARDOZO KINDERSLEY CAMBRIDGE 2001

Photo: Michael Nedo

Copyright © 1966, 1976 David Kindersley & 2001 Lida Lopes Cardozo Kindersley
British Library Cataloguing in Publication Data available
ISBN 1 874426 13 9

First published 1966
Second revised edition 1976 published by The Wynkyn de Worde Society
Third edition 2001 published by Cardozo Kindersley

All rights reserved. No part of this publication may be reproduced in any form without prior permission from the publisher.

Copies of this or any other Cardozo Kindersley publication are available from
The Cardozo Kindersley Workshop
152 Victoria Road, Cambridge CB4 3DZ, UK
Telephone 01223 362170

Designed by Dale Tomlinson, using the series layout designed by Eiichi Kono.
Edited and produced by Lida Lopes Cardozo Kindersley
Printed by BAS Printers Limited UK
Illustrations are from the Cardozo Kindersley Archives & p.14 Michael Manni Photographic

The body text has been set in 12 pt Emilida, a typeface designed by Lida Lopes Cardozo Kindersley, digitised by ITA Kono Design and commissioned by Timothy Guy Design for EMI

Contents

David Kindersley's vision 6
Foreword by Francis Cave 7

The beginning 15
Optical centres 17
Our first instrument for spacing 20
A more scientific approach 22
The eye 25
Spacing by eye 29
New methods of printing need new methods of spacing 34
Lower case 35
Initial capital and lower case 36
A design tool 37
The influence of calligraphy 39
Possible economy in better spacing 40
Two kinds of spacing 43
An optical spacing instrument in use 44
Ten years later 48
Revised graph 49
Computerised centres 52
Italics 56
Conclusion 58

Bibliography 60

David Kindersley's vision

The proper spacing of alphabets of capitals and lower case should be such that the texture of the printed page is even. A glance at a fifth-century Rustic Roman letter (1) will show this principle in operation long ago. As will a vigorous fifteenth-century printing by Peter Schöffer (2), and the printing (1471) by Nicholas Jenson (3). By good spacing I mean, quite simply, that each letter should appear to be exactly in the centre between its two neighbours. To me this is the only criterion, and I do not believe that it requires any further justification. Put another way, any letter should occupy a passive position between its neighbours.

Foreword by Francis Cave

David Kindersley first approached me about his system of optical letter spacing in 1984. By then his belief that the computer could be a powerful tool for mechanically determining the correct optical spacing of any letterform had already received a significant boost through the work of a team of computer science graduates led by Dr Neil Wiseman and David Kindersley at the Cambridge University Computing Laboratory. Their work had led to the first practical, computer-based implementation of the system, using a Linotype Omnitech 2000 (the first laser-based digital phototypesetter to be sold commercially) connected to a computer programmed to calculate the correct optical spacing for its set of 'bitmap' fonts. The same computer was also used to compose text, using the optically spaced fonts, and drive the Omnitech to produce text galleys on rolls of photographic paper. The development of this system continued until 1986 and was used thereafter to support David's efforts to find a commercial application for the system. The Omnitech system was occasionally used in the Workshop on lettering projects, and in 1989 it was used to typeset the book David Kindersley: His Work and Workshop, published by Cardozo Kindersley Editions.

> For the composition of this publication about the work of David Kindersley the type face 'Optima' was used in connection with David Kindersley's LOGOS spacing program. As demonstrated here, with phototypesetting you have the possibility of perfect intercharacter spacing.

An example of David's spacing in practice, typeset in Hermann Zapf's Optima for 'David Kindersley: His Work and Workshop' by Montague Shaw.

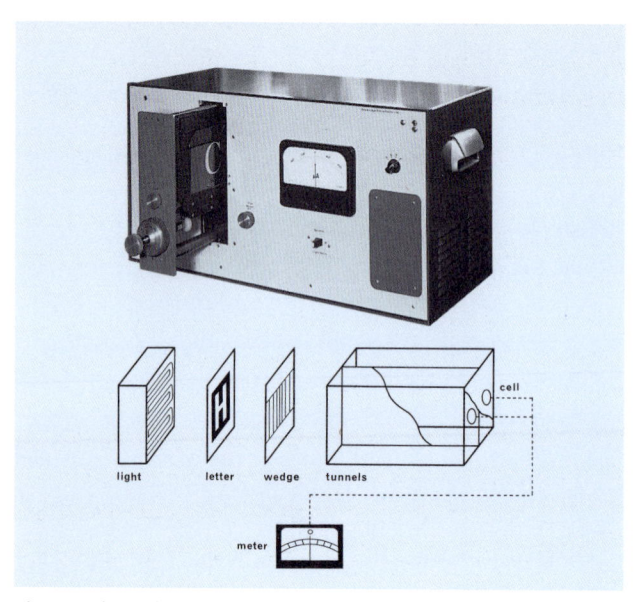

The original optical letter spacing machine built by Cambridge Consultants in the 1960s to David's design.

My role in all this was originally that of an external consultant. Following a recommendation from his friend Roy Fullick, David had approached Pira, the UK research and information centre for the printing and publishing industries, for advice on commercial exploitation of the system. I was one of the consultancy team at Pira who responded to David's enquiry. Once I understood the tremendous potential of the system to improve the quality of phototypesetting (I don't remember being a convert overnight!), I enthusiastically set about assisting David to publicise his ideas and what had already been achieved. Surely a system that would not only provide improved legibility but also, by allowing for more precise and therefore tighter spacing, make more efficient use of the printed area of a page or screen, would find favour everywhere.

However, neither David nor I had reckoned on the extent to which the typesetting industry was wedded to the status quo, in other words: a spacing system based upon rectangular 'bounding boxes' and, in an attempt to overcome the inadequacies of this method, tables of 'kerning' adjustments that in many cases the users of a typesetting system were expected to set up for themselves. Impressed though many were by the results that David was achieving, they mostly remained unconvinced that the system offered sufficient tangible benefits to outweigh the admittedly substantial costs of making radical changes to their system software at that time.

When, in 1986, development of the Omnitech system by Dr Wiseman's team ceased, it had already been clear to David for some time that, while much had been achieved with the system, there was more work still to be done. The Omnitech system was producing better spacing than conventional typesetting systems, but had been optimised for a limited range of type styles. The principles of optical spacing – that each letterform defines its own optical centre and its own 'intrinsic width', and that the correct spacing of letterforms is to be determined by making the distance between the optical centres of neighbouring letterforms equal to half the intrinsic width of each letterform plus a constant – had been clearly shown to work. But it was still not certain that the best algorithm for calculating the optical centre and intrinsic width of an arbitrary letterform had been identified. I therefore decided to take on the task of searching for an improved algorithm.

David with Dr Wiseman's team had tried a variety of formulae for calculating and balancing the optical 'weight' of a letterform, and had eventually settled upon one that involved fourth-power moments, weighted by a diamond-shaped wedge. However, formulae involving higher-power moments had been tried and had achieved good results in some circumstances, and there was still the feeling that the curved shape of an elliptical wedge was theoretically more likely to be correct than a diamond.

Another layer of uncertainty concerned the use of a 'canonical' letterform, an idealised, geometric shape used in calculating the 'intrinsic width' of a letterform. The method of calculating the intrinsic width using the canonical was as follows. Having calculated the optical weight of a letterform, using a specific formula, the horizontal width of the canonical would be adjusted until its own optical weight converged on that of the letterform. The intrinsic width of a letterform was defined to be the horizontal width of a canonical of equal optical weight.

A further uncertainty about the soundness of the algorithms employed in the Omnitech system lay in the fact that different algorithms were being used to calculate the optical centre and the optical weight of the same letterform.

When I started searching for an improved algorithm in 1986, I decided that it would be most practical, given the technologies around at the time and the specific resources available to me, to base my work upon the low-resolution fonts and electrophotographic imaging method of a laserprinter. Whatever worked in that environment could reasonably be expected to work at least as well with the high-resolution fonts and photochemical imaging method of a phototypesetter.

Driven by the necessity to re-write the software to suit these new circumstances, I had the opportunity to return to the basic idea of optical spacing that David had articulated long before: that the correct spacing of a letterform can be calculated purely from the letterform itself using a single formula. In discussion with David it became clear that it had been his goal all along to implement this basic idea, but that practical constraints in the construction of the earlier optical-mechanical spacing system had made it impossible to implement. The design of the Omnitech system was derived from the successful optical-mechanical system, but this led to a number of features of the opto-mechanical system being implemented in the computer-based system, despite the opportunity to abandon these constraints. There is a curious analogy here with the way that modern typesetting software remains tethered to the rectangular bounding boxes that have been inherited from the constraints of the earlier technology for setting type as lines of 'lead soldiers'. The design of the Omnitech system, in both David's and my opinion, owed too much to its opto-mechanical antecedent and had not gone back sufficiently to first principles.

Intermittently between 1986 and 1988 David and I carried on the search for an improved formula. Regrettably, changes in my work circumstances towards the end of 1988 meant that I was unable to continue, but the results up to that point had been encouraging. I had produced some creditable results for letterform in various styles (serif and sans serif styles, upright and sloped). I had abandoned the canonical without this impeding further progress. I had achieved some encouraging results with an elliptical wedge. I had developed a single formula, based upon the elliptical wedge and fourth-power moments, for calculating both the optical centre and the intrinsic width, which appeared to work equally well (albeit not perfectly) on all letterforms. As a result I believe firmly that David's original goal of finding a single formula that works for all letterforms is achievable.

The challenges now, as I see it, are not only to perfect the formula for calculating optical centres and intrinsic widths – I have no doubt that this can be achieved, whether or not the end result will bear any exact relationship to what has been achieved in the past – but also to apply this to the full gamut of text presentation tasks performed in print and on computer screen today.

In my opinion, the formula that meets these challenges will be able to trace its ancestry directly back to David Kindersley's original work. His long consideration of the nature and process of making judgements about good spacing not only convinced him that there had to be a single formula that would work but also enabled him to refine and improve the reliability of his own judgement. The system was working inside his head – we must therefore continue the hunt for the elusive formula that he applied to such amazingly good effect.

I believe that a full implementation of David's system will have the most profoundly beneficial effects in circumstances where text is at present being spaced particularly poorly, such as on computer screens and on other low-resolution imaging devices such as ink jet and laser printers, where correct spacing is crucial to optimising legibility. But there is a general need for better spacing. In his postscript to the book by Montague Shaw that was typeset using David's system, Hermann Zapf puts it this way:

> *"Today with our modern phototypesetting systems we should be able to get the most perfect intercharacter spacing. But why do we still see so many bad examples everywhere? There is a perfect letterspacing program already available, David Kindersley's spacing program, which I would like to see become an industrial standard and adapted to all typesetting systems. It is very important, and furthermore it is needed."*

What is needed now is for someone who has read this book, and been convinced by its arguments, to take up the challenge of finding the formula that works for all letterforms. To do this will involve further research and development, and I believe that a necessary starting point for this will be to obtain the fullest possible understanding of the work that has already been done by David.

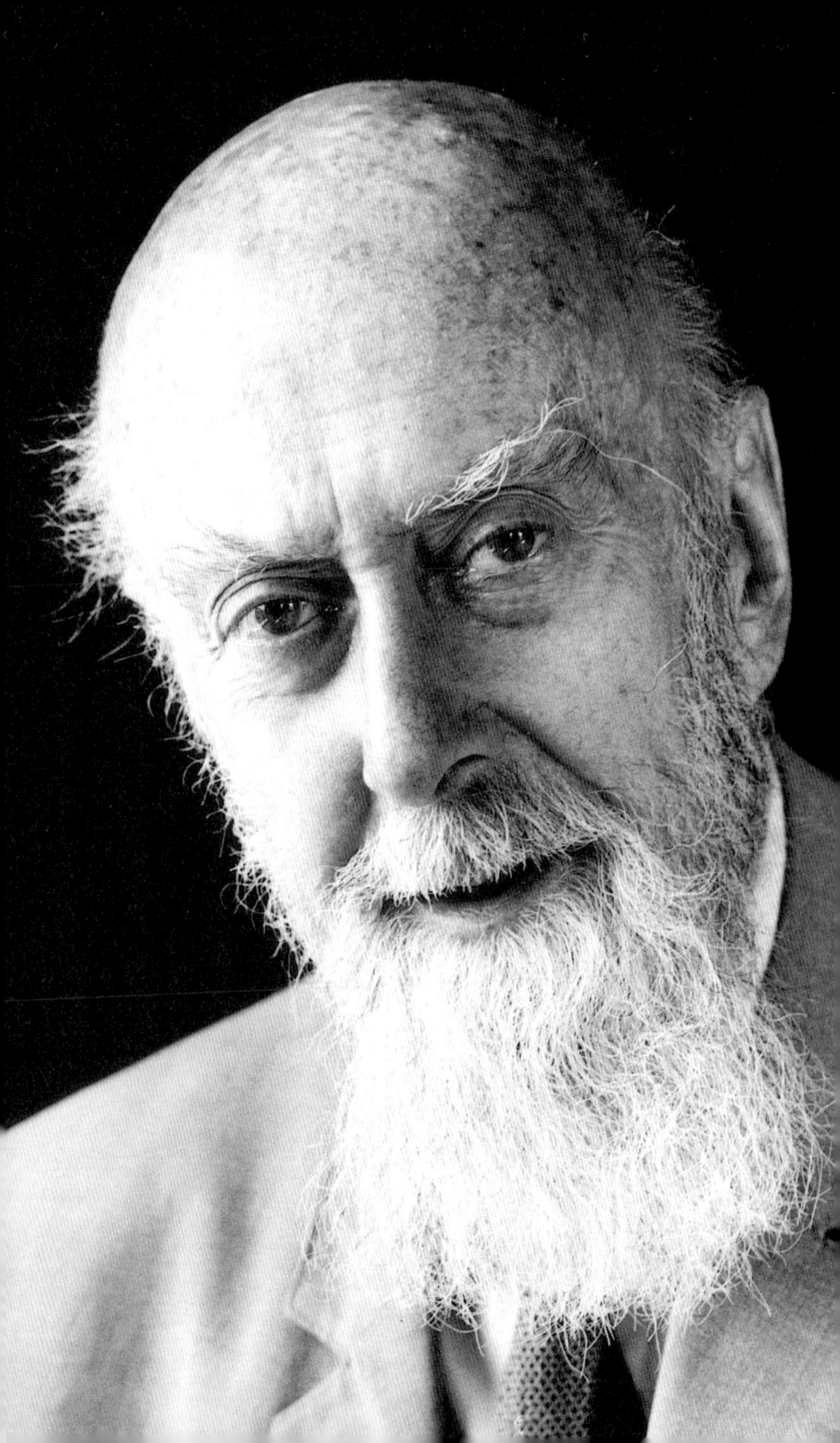

The beginning

Shortly after the war, I think in 1947, Mr Crutchley, the University Printer, and I were horrified to wake up one morning to find the unique and characterful cast-iron street names being removed from the centre of Cambridge. Furthermore they were being replaced by a particularly bad sample of Ministry of Transport lettering – equally badly spaced. It was believed that the new street signs were more legible and thus the change was justified. All praise goes to the City Engineer, who promptly put back the cast-iron signs when it was pointed out that at least it was doubtful whether the new signs were more legible than the old. Unfortunately the patterns from which the cast-iron signs were cast had ceased to be available and new streets and roads required name-plates. So it came about that I 'set-to-work' designing a street name alphabet (Fig. 1).

Fig. 1

My first task was to visit the sign makers and to find out how signs were made. By and large my design took into account the limitations of casting and particularly stamping, but the main feature was the built-in system of spacing. Here was the greatest need. It can truly be said that sign makers who were producing direction signs, street nameplates and car numbers had, at that time, no idea of spacing at all (Fig. 2).

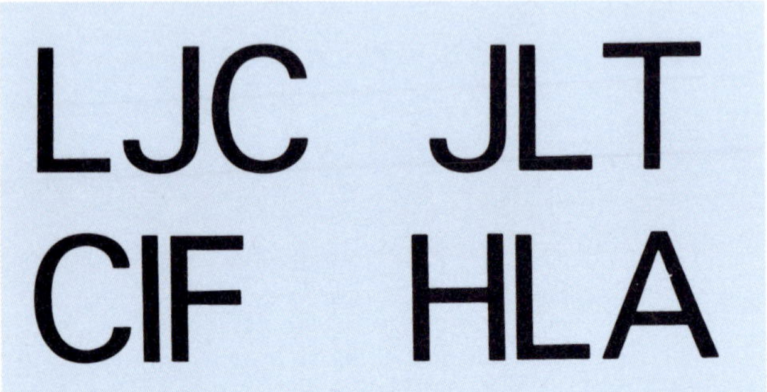

LJC JLT
CIF HLA

Fig. 2

This in part was due to a directive from the Ministry of Transport who stated that no letter should be closer than ½ inch on car number plates. At the same time it must be pointed out that the letters illustrated appear as they would if set solid in type. In other words an example, more or less, of spacing based on the widths of letters. My completed design for a street name alphabet was turned down by the Cambridge Council and a fierce correspondence arose in the local press. Ultimately my alphabet plus systems of spacing for two other alphabets – 'Gill Sans' and 'Standard M.o.T.' – were bought by the Ministry of Transport. Without realizing it Cambridge chose my alphabet out of a catalogue and after all my signs gradually appeared in the streets!

This, then, was the beginning of my interest in the spacing of alphabets by eye so that all letters would fit together automatically whatever order was chosen. Whilst engaged on my street name alphabet I formed a very strong opinion that I was only scratching at the problem of letter-spacing, and that somewhere deeper than I could see for the moment there was a set of rules that could be applied to all alphabets, and perhaps all symbols that were arranged laterally, and that these rules if closely parallel to the function of the eye would achieve good spacing. This is the really important thing – the eye – how does it balance, how does it space; and yet this is not all, because what we know of spacing seems directly to contradict the simple interpretation of the image on the retina. The cerebral cortex perhaps only uses the retinal image and then blends this information with experience received from the other senses.

Optical centres

It was many years before I could again return to the problems of optical spacing. In fact the first 'credit squeeze' produced cancellations of commissions which gave me the time to return again to the task. I believe it was 1961 when we started endlessly counting the millimetre squares on graph paper that fell within the bounds of letters. I wanted to know what happened if spacing were directly related to letter area (Fig.3).

CCDDFFIIJJLLMMOOPP

CCDDFFIIJJLLMMOOPP

CCDDFFIIJJLLMMOOPP

Fig. 3

Here we have
(1) optical spacing and centres;
(2) letter width spacing;
(3) area spacing and area centres.

No joy here, and yet there was something. In this particular alphabet some letters had the same area but obviously they could not have the same space. Moreover they did not express the eye-preferred centres when the area was divided equally on either side of a vertical line. I had already learned from my previous attempts at automatic eye-spacing that the problem of spacing fell into two parts. Firstly the correct space area expressed by the letter itself had to be found and secondly the correct position of the letter in its own space depended on the eye-chosen vertical centre (Fig. 4).

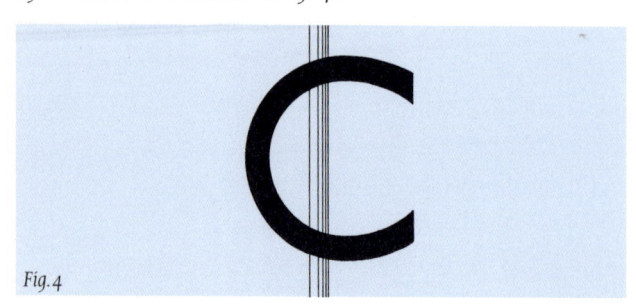

Fig. 4

In this 'C' the optical centre is very near the third moment centre and the mathematical centre. The mathematical centre is equidistant between the left and right projections of a letter (including serifs). The other centres are, from the left: (1) area; (2) first moment (gravity); (3) second moment (inertia); (4) third moment (optical?); (5) mathematical centre or the vertical halfway between the left and right projections of the letter.

The optical centre must coincide with the mathematical centre of the space. These two factors, the correct space and the correct optical centre, alone provide the key to interchangeability of characters. At this time I could see no way of finding the optical centre except by eye, so I continued with trying to find the space first – in the hope that in the middle of some night the centre problem would be answered! 'C's were not behaving at all well as regards centres. We were getting, of course, the area centre. Whereas the kind of centres required by the eye are shown on the Baskerville 'L' & 'C'. You can see the problem. It indeed looked insoluble (Fig. 5).

Fig. 5

Returning to the letters that had the same area. It seemed reasonable to suppose that the rectangular quality of say the 'B' as opposed to the more overall square shape of the 'H' should be allowed to reflect in its space, in spite of their area equality. A further trial with some other letters led me to the same conclusion. Though this conclusion is only partly true, it did lead me farther along the trail. With the help of an engineer we made up a small gadget which made rectangles of the exact size in which a letter would fit. We counted all the millimetre squares in the letter and then reduced the rectangle in exact proportions until the same number of squares could be counted within the rectangle. This was hard labour but we found the result satisfactory.

Our first instrument for spacing

Soon we were measuring our letters by transmitted light and a photo-electric cell, and then reducing the characteristic rectangle to give the same light value. These rectangles came to be known as letter blocks, and by adding a constant to their lateral width we were able to achieve reasonable spacing. But of course we still had to position the letters by eye within their spaces.

Having by now learned a little about light sources and photo-electric cells – it occurred to us that the centres might be found if some kind of light wedge was put over the letter so as to exclude light from its vertical centre but permit light with increasing intensity to pass through either side. And by moving the letter to and fro from left to right under this wedge, it could become positioned where at least the light was balanced. This seemed to have promise, and although we still did not get the eye-preferred centres we were looking for, we did get centres that tended away from area and towards the required optical centres (Fig. 6).

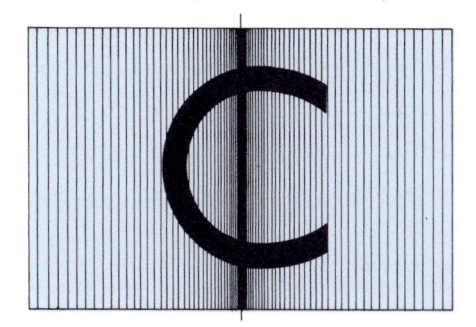

Fig. 6

Suddenly, it dawned on me that the finding of centres and the spaces were one and the same thing. Find the right centres and you will then have in light value terms, through the wedge, the correct space. In theory we were getting somewhere. In fact none of us had the technique of making wedges. Kodak would make us wedges if we told them what sort of wedge we wanted! It would be expensive anyway!

Then started the long nightmare of wedge-making. First painting them on pieces of film actually over the letter to see how it moved the centre. At one time we made tanks out of three sheets of glass glued with Araldite and filled them with inky water measuring the amount of ink to water. The photographer was not amused when the tank burst in an upstairs room above his shop! Next we constructed about 100 thin strips of card carefully graded by painting from white to black. We then photographed them to make a wedge. But alas, nothing quite worked. Should the wedge be circular? It seemed a good idea, and surely the eye more truly matches this approach, but the results were worse. For this purpose we cast wedges in brass matrices with gelatine and dye. The first signs of hysteria were setting in!

A more scientific approach

A new approach to wedge-making must be found, we said. Fortunately Dr Colin Quinn came to our aid. He gave us precise calculations for different progressions so that we were able to make large wedges on Bristol board with a ruling pen. By this means we made very accurate first, second and third moment progression wedges and our third moment wedge began to show the way.

By the nature of its construction the wedge was very dark. Undaunted, Dr Quinn recalculated the wedge so that we could construct it out of circles, thus enabling us to get more accurate readings towards its centre. The illustration is of a second moment wedge made in this way (Fig. 7).

Fig. 7

You may wonder why a bunch of amateurs without any kind of scientific training failed to approach people professionally engaged in the problems confronting us. The answer is that we did as far as we were able, but I'm afraid on the whole people are not inclined to help if they do not think the project will work or if they feel no necessity for it. Not so though with Dr Quinn. At least he kept an open mind and through his guidance and discipline we more or less started all over again.

Dr Quinn made me do two things. Firstly he pointed out that as professional letterers we might have all kinds of built-in prejudices as regards spacing which could at least partly be ruled out if we spaced symbols which we had not previously spaced. Secondly, with the same set of symbols he suggested ways of finding out whether or not wider or narrower spacing was the result of adding or subtracting a constant (Fig. 8).

Fig. 8

The illustration shows in the top three lines the results of eye-spacing. The method of spacing was as follows. Two squares were placed at a set distance apart in the centre of a large white board and on either side all the other symbols were arranged and rearranged until several answers were obtained for every combination of symbols. The experiment was repeated several times. In each series the squares were set closer. As can be seen the spacing reduces in a constant fashion and in this experiment there was no sign of a proportional decrease.

The lower line is an example of putting the same symbols through the instrument such as it was at that time.

One small and perhaps significant detail worth drawing your attention to is that a triangle with its apex at the top tended to require more space than a triangle the other way. I have not really found this reiterated in letters. For example the 'A' and 'V', but then the impact on the retina is considerably less forceful. But it shows clearly enough that one must not necessarily expect the same spacing if symbols are placed upside down.

By now we had evolved a fairly reliable instrument for working with. For example, we had achieved a tolerably even area of light from a multi-light source of small bulbs and we had ironed out an optical system to bring all the light that passed through the letter onto a photo-cell. We made up films of alphabets so that a letter could be passed back and forth over the light wedge until the light was balanced on each side. But we still did not possess the perfect wedge, and it may well be that being a perfectionist I never shall. It depends on how obsessional one is. About this time I was shown how to make wedges by mechanically moving a mask or profile across a piece of film, and although I now know what must surely be the best way of all, we are still using this method.

The eye

Naturally enough I've read and digested what I can about the eye, but it is immensely complicated (Fig. 9). I should perhaps remind you that there are about 130,000,000 receptors in the retina of the eye. The peripheral parts of the retina are more sensitive than the central part of the eye, which is more accurate. The receptors in the periphery tend to be in groups of rods belonging to a single optic fibre, whereas the cones in the fovea tend to be connected singly to their optic fibres, and thus have a more direct line to the brain. My own feeling is that the centre of a letter would result from a simple progression if it were left to the peripheral vision. But though this seems to be chiefly so, the fovea, which is about a third of a millimetre across, just alters the results obtained by the great bulk of the eye's receptors in the periphery. Further the fovea appears to affect the letters at their tops. It is well known and easily verified that the eye, at least when reading, centres its vision just along the top line of the lettering, be they capital letters or lower case x height.

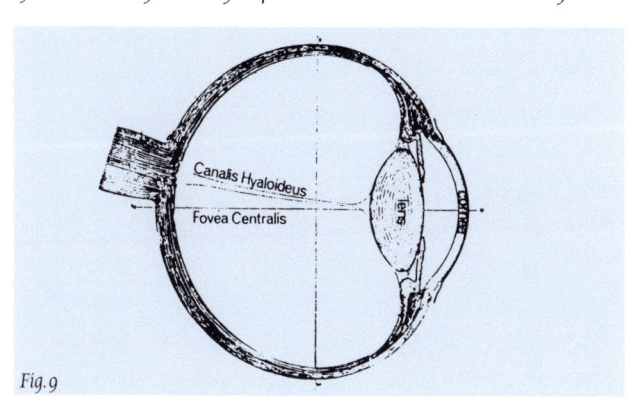

Fig. 9

The centring of vision seems, as I say, to follow the top line of the x height of lower case, and from a spacing point of view ascenders do not contribute at all, as can be seen in the illustrations (Figs. 10, 11 and 12).

Fig. 10

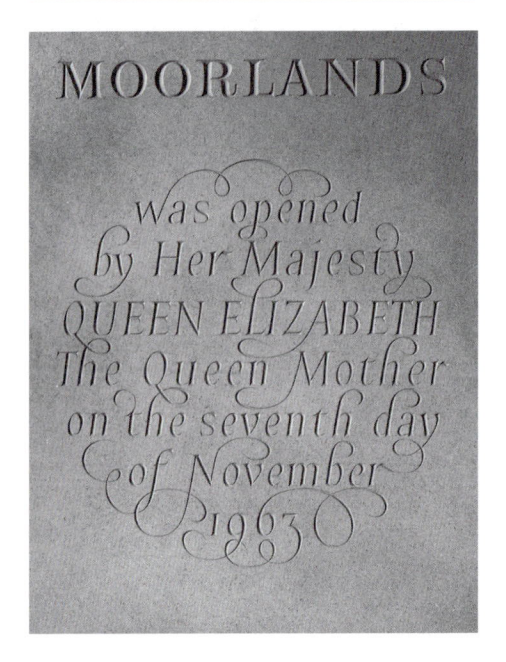

Fig. 11

Fig. 12

That the eye does this can be ascertained by forming an impression on the retina by looking at a bright light through a small hole. There is time to see the resulting small counter impression or dot move along the top of the lettering as one reads. It is certainly true that the characteristic and differentiating parts of letters lie in the main in the top half. But I feel this is not the reason for the preference of the eye to centre along the top, and that man has unconsciously designed letters with their main features of recognition near the top to comply with the way the eye behaves. The reason

may be just that we are flat worms crawling around the earth with our visual world divided between dark earth and light sky and we settle for the horizon! Another factor in the eye which requires coming to terms with is simultaneous contrast. Put very simply this is the stimulus of receptors adjacent to the image on the retina. White is whiter than white immediately next to black. When spacing is too close this intensity increase might erode the image.

As I saw the problem of spacing at this time, all we needed was an instrument capable of balancing letters not on their centre of gravity, but perhaps nearer to a third moment centre. (Figs. 13, 14 and 15). As shown below, we visualized the problem in this way. The 'm' at the bottom is balanced on its correct fulcrum. The slanting 'iki' is type-set whilst the horizontal version is optically set.

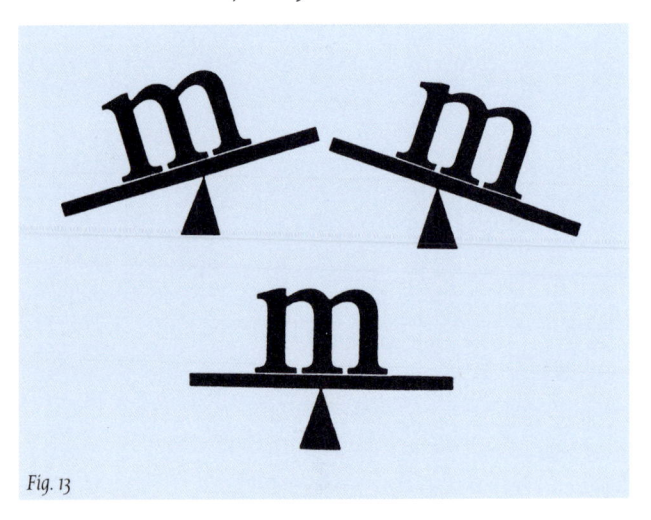

Fig. 13

Figs. 14 and 15

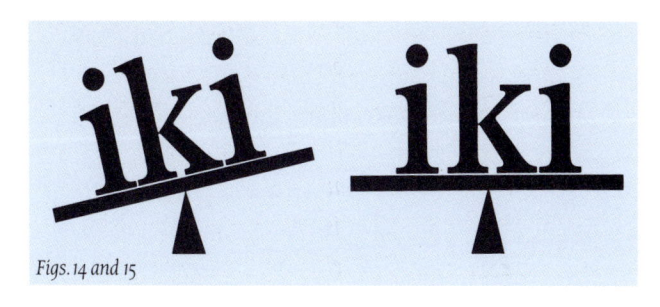

Spacing by eye

Whilst trying to make an instrument that would assess the space values and centres of letters in a way similar to the eye we have become far more adept at spacing by eye. In the first place one must space many alphabets before one can be sure that there is a common factor.

Alphabets must continuously be tried against a new light wedge. Thus it is possible to see from the amount of scatter on the graph how wrong the wedge is (Fig. 16). Ideal conditions

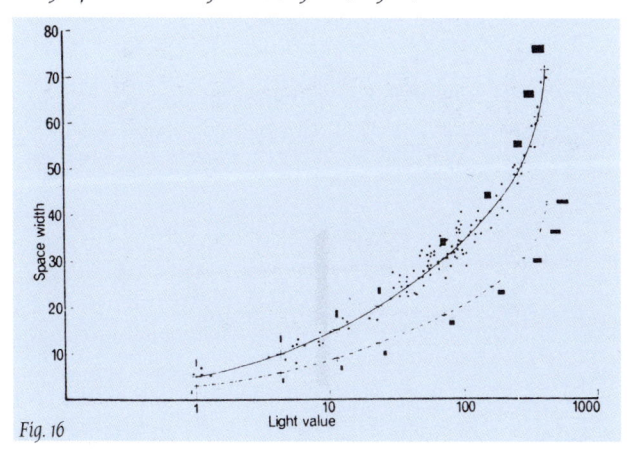

Fig. 16

i.e. a perfect set of eye calculations and a wedge conforming to the visual stimulus of the eye, will produce a smooth line which we would call a space curve. All alphabets will space along the same line providing for the purposes of our instrument they have the same height. The line can be raised or lowered in parallel to correspond with the minimum fit of the most asymmetrical letter with the smallest value, generally the capital 'L'.

As stated above we can now space alphabets by eye quickly and accurately. The method is to set up 'O' and 'I' of the alphabet at an arbitrary distance apart, and to the right of the 'O' 'I' place yet another 'I' and adjust until the first 'I' looks evenly spaced (Fig. 17).

OI OII

Fig. 17

Now we have to place to the right of the 'O' 'I' 'I' an 'I' 'O' having exactly the same distance between them as the 'O' 'I' on the left (Fig. 18).

OIIIO

Fig. 18

In the illustration it will be seen that the 'I' 'O' has been adjusted as a unit until the centre 'I' is in the middle. Here we have the opportunity to move the 'O' 'I' and 'I' 'O' apart if we feel the three 'I's are giving too dense a colour.

Clearly we can now easily ascertain the space for the 'I's by bisecting the distance between them and consequently, we can find the space for the 'O' (Fig. 19).

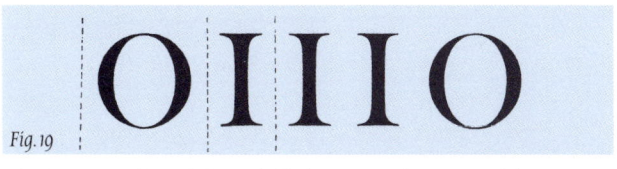

Fig. 19

The 'L' was selected first of all characters because of the relationship between its optical space and its shape. Due to its asymmetrical shape the 'L' has its optical centre far removed from its mathematical centre with the result that on a condensed setting it is the character most likely to kern (i.e. overhang its own space).

For practical reasons kerning is undesirable in the initial stages of determining relative optical spaces for characters. Therefore close setting which would produce this is to be avoided. In the other direction because errors in spacing are less noticeable when characters are widely set – a wide set is also to be avoided. The ideal working set therefore would be when the 'L' is provided with the minimum space without any part of it projecting beyond its space (Fig. 20).

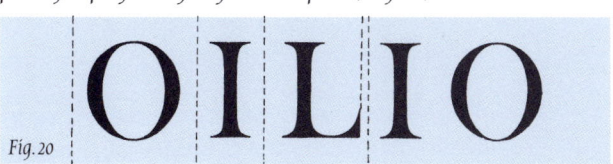

Fig. 20

The minimum 'L' fit therefore is the distance between the optical centre of the 'L' and the farthest right-hand extremity multiplied by two.

One is now ready to make the last adjustment to 'I' 'O' before going ahead with the other letters. It is, as I have said, likely that the 'L' will prove to be the letter that sets the minimum true spacing of the alphabet. It is as well to adjust the 'O' 'I' and 'I' 'O' so that the 'L' neither projects into their space nor has any slack.

Remember that we have satisfactorily proved that spacing can be increased or decreased by a constant. Remember the square and triangle, etc. So it is a relatively simple job to alter the 'I's and 'O's to the 'L' (Fig. 21). At the same time we must mark the optical centres.

Fig. 21

Now we can go ahead and place each letter in turn between our set 'O' 'I' and 'I' 'O' units, operating them to and fro until the spacing looks right (Fig. 22).

Fig. 22

Remembering to measure the distance between the two 'I' spaces to ascertain the space value of the letter being assessed and mark the optical centre on each letter which will, of course, coincide with the half-distance measured.

Providing all is done carefully you will be able to arrange these letters in any order and the spacing will remain good (Fig. 23).

ABCDEFGHI
JKLMNOPQR
STUVWXYZ

Fig. 23

Perhaps it is high time that I explained what I mean by good spacing. Quite simply I mean that each letter should appear to be exactly in the centre between its two neighbours. To me this is the only criterion, and I do not believe that it requires any further justification. Put another way, any letter should occupy a passive position between its neighbours such as the top example (Fig. 24). The middle example is as type set. The bottom example is based on area.

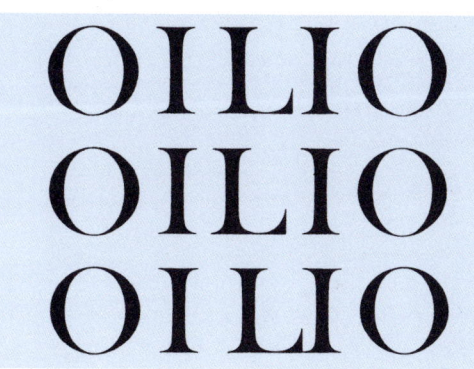

OILIO
OILIO
OILIO

Fig. 24

New methods of printing need new methods of spacing

Did a sense of spacing gradually depart as the scriptorium ceased to exercise its influence on the printer? And did it receive its final blow as engineers produced their ever more marvellous printing presses, but which could not deal with more than a certain number of variables as regards unit spaces? It is surely true that the calligrapher had reached a very high standard of spacing at the advent of printing, and that the first printers were not satisfied unless their work was as fine as the calligrapher's. The layman would be hard pressed to tell the difference!

We now have an entirely new set of circumstances with the onset of photo-printing. No hard and fast barrier need exist between letters. Letter-spacing can once again reign. Each space can be the direct expression of each character. That is the positioning of a letter in its correct optical space on the optical fulcrum or centre. This is of immense importance to the undisturbed scanning of the printed line of words by the human eye.

On the other hand it is possible given certain unit widths to design an alphabet tailored precisely to those widths. A lateral width of space of a certain amount means in fact a symbol of an exactly related light value, centred and taken under the light wedge. In other words it seems that the unit width, whether predetermined or not, must be exactly related to the letter and be the expression of a certain intensity of image received by the retina.

Solid images such as rectangles all of the same height respond in the same way. For example brickwork (Fig. 25), whether

Fig. 25

headers or stretchers or any other length. It is not spaced nicely if the jointing varies. It strikes me as extremely interesting that varying width rectangles of the same height can be accurately measured and spaced on the graph (Fig. 16).

Lower case

So far I have dealt chiefly with capital letters. Obviously they are by far the most difficult to space of the two alphabets that we use – capitals and lower case. The greater differentiation between capital letters accounts for much of the variation in spaces. Whilst the extremes are greater in the lower case 'i' and 'm' there are more letters nearly the same. Nevertheless, lower case responds to exactly the same treatment as the capital letters, and because our daily reading fodder is in lower case, its spacing is even more important.

When we are concerned with optical spacing, regardless of whether we are dealing in letters or some other form of symbol and providing all characters are brought to a common height, the growth rate of space remains the same. It is the weight of the symbol, together with the dispersal of that weight measured in ever increasing terms outwards on either side of the optical position, which gives you the symbol's allotted space.

It would, of course, be possible but very difficult to make light wedges for every varying x height. But it is much more practical to keep the wedge a constant size (like a fixed eye) and make all our symbols conform to the same height, thus in a sense varying the letter size rather than the eye.

To obtain the correct spacing for the lower case is just a question of dividing the capital space curve on the graph according to the small x height relation of lower case to capitals. Thus the light values for lower case of two-thirds capital height are plotted on the lower line and space readings are taken off the left of the graph in a similar fashion to the capitals. (This is now not considered to be true. Stroke thickness is taken into account. See page 50).

Initial capital and lower case

The capital initial set to lower case is not an easy one to solve satisfactorily, but I don't think there is any necessity to make a capital alphabet especially for this purpose as is normally the case, as capitals to be spaced properly must then be done by eye.

Some alternative settings are needed if the optical setting of capitals to lower case is to be satisfactory (Fig. 26). For example, the 'T' must have on its right a closer fit when followed by a lower case letter of x height than when the lower case letter has

Fig. 26

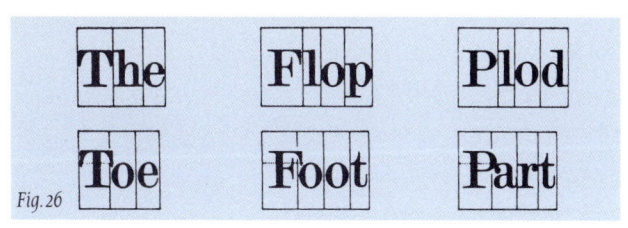

an ascender on its left. This means, in effect, that the eye is judging the 'T' in the first instance as a lower case letter with an ascending top, and in the second instance the lower case letter as a capital and therefore including the ascender.

This principle may extend in some alphabets to the other capital letters that are wider above the small x height than below. At the most they are few in number and need alternative sets on the right side only. The capitals likely to need special treatment are 'F' 'P' 'T' 'V' 'W' 'Y'.

A design tool

The design of letters can be greatly helped by an instrument such as the one incorporating my ideas, which is made by Mr Southward, of Cambridge Consultants Ltd, for Letraset Ltd, the makers of dry transfer lettering. Whilst its use for the moment is to facilitate the placing of spacing markers or guides on sheets of Letraset it could contribute very greatly to the design of letters, and particularly to their fit within a predetermined unit width.

To be concerned with the proper fit of letters, one to another, in a way pleasing and economical is only reasonable. Earlier we noticed that the optical set of an alphabet tended to be limited by the capital 'L' (Fig. 27).

The illustration shows in a purely theoretical way how the 'L' can be modified to occupy a smaller space, firstly by reducing the projection of the horizontal stroke, and secondly by increasing the weight at the tip of the horizontal stroke. It can be seen straight away that the shift in the optical centre in the third example decreases the space requirements of the 'L' in spite of adding to its area. Many of the more fanciful Victorian display types seem to sense the need for bringing the optical centre over as near to the mathematical centre as possible. The secret of a good fit and an economical one lies precisely in moving the optical centre towards the mathematical centre.

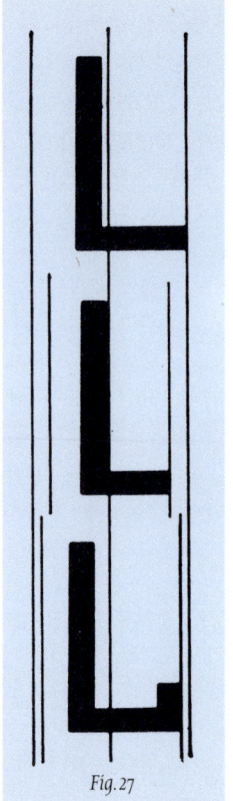

Fig. 27

This is only one way the machine has of influencing the design of letters. Another is in guiding the designer to produce a letter in complete accord with its space.

As I have already stated, the space allotted to any character must ideally be an expression of that character. Therefore it would also be true that, if the space is predetermined, the letter must be an expression of the space. In other words, the intensity of two characters that are to occupy similar spaces must be equal for the retina. This does not mean, of course, that the designs must be similar, but that their weight expressed in moment terms around a centre must be equal. If therefore it is desirable to produce an alphabet with only six different unit widths, it is equally desirable that the letters have only six different weights, if spacing and colour are considered important.

To be asked as a designer to alter his design from this point of view seems to me to be something he would understand and wish to do. But to be told simply to narrow or expand the letter to occupy a larger or smaller unit width is not any longer quite good enough, particularly when the end result does not seem quite to justify it.

The influence of calligraphy

I have always been mesmerized by good calligraphy. Not only is there the marvellous co-ordination of hand, eye, and attention to watch in the good calligrapher at work, but there is the further miracle of spacing. We with predetermined letter forms have no excuse for bad spacing – in theory we can move our letters about until they look right, or do it all again. The calligrapher must do it right the first time. And by right we mean shape his letters and space them at the same time. This he does in an apparently effortless manner. What judgement! We have been talking about putting any one letter in a passive position between any two. The calligrapher has the very remarkable talent of placing a letter where it will be in the passive position between two, but only when he has put down the third letter. Little things may please little minds, but this certainly pleases me! To make things still more complicated the calligrapher can expand or condense his letter forms in the minutest way in order to justify his text. Indeed in the last analysis 'justifying' can only be done if everything is modified, lettershape and space. For me justifying has no validity in type, except for space margins between columns. I prefer a ragged right-hand margin and cannot believe that all the difficulties involved in justification are really worth while. The recent examples of this in Design magazine seemed to me delightful.

Possible economy in better spacing

Perfect spacing means that the letters in a word are bonded like bricks, and therefore maximum word pattern recognition is possible with no cause for the eye to be arrested in its scanning on account of spacing. Moreover because of the uniformity of the spacing inter-letter-wise it is possible to open the spacing only slightly to achieve word separation. Thus producing a closer knit text altogether than is necessitated at present.

Here is an example of type set above and the letters and words re-spaced below (Fig. 28). Note the extra area needed for the

**Designers Deserve
More Opportunity**

**Designers Deserve
More Opportunity**

Fig. 28

lower example, which is by no means always the case with optical spacing. This is an example again of type set solid revealing a poor texture (Fig. 29) and next we have the same letters spaced more correctly and reduced in size to occupy the same area as the previous illustration (Fig. 30).

abcdefghijklmnopqrst
uvwxyzabcdefghijklm
nopqrstuvwxyzabcdef
ghijklmnopqrstuvwxy
zabcdefghijklmnopqrs
tuvwxyz

Fig. 29

abcdefghijklmnopqrst
uvwxyzabcdefghijklmn
opqrstuvwxyzabcdefgh
ijklmnopqrstuvwxyzab
cdefghijklmnopqrstuv
wxyzabcdefghijklmnop
qrstuvwxyz

Fig. 30

Is there any loss of legibility? Recent research undertaken by Dr Poulton at Cambridge in conjunction with the Council of Industrial Design confirms one's belief that letter differentiation is a strong clue to the achievement of a greater comprehensibility of type matter. The results of his research showed, amongst the types tested, no real difference between a good sans serif and a good seriffed type. However, it did show Gill Sans Medium to be statistically superior to other sans serif faces. This type is both classical and geometrical in design – two good reasons why it made such a good showing. There is, however, one other factor, that may or may not have contributed to its comprehensibility factor. And that is its spacing. It has a markedly wider set for all its narrower letters than the other sans serif types, against which it was tested, and this, in spite of its considerably smaller x height, has played its part. Is this Univers more or less comprehensible if optically spaced? Fig. 31 is typeset, whereas Fig. 32 is optically spaced by 'the optical letter spacer'. Note that both versions occupy the same area.

Another reason for supposing a greater degree of legibility when the spacing is controlled in a direct relation to characters has come to light in the field of traffic direction signs. The image on the retina of a 12 inch letter seen at a considerable distance is not so very different to very small type at normal reading distance. It is reasonable to suppose that the wider spacing so necessary for a direction sign is also required in reading matter. As can be clearly shown in Dr Poulton's research, the wider spacing of the Gill Sans Medium has not

> **must be carried by some**
> **own free will this devo**
> **allow himself to be bitte**
> **drawing some of his own**
> **three other members of th**
> **selfless devotion.**

Fig. 31

> **must be carried by some**
> **own free will this devote**
> **allow himself to be bitte**
> **drawing some of his owr**
> **three other members of**
> **selfless devotion.**

Fig. 32

meant an increase in the area covered by the type – on the contrary it is less. It is reasonable, therefore, to suppose that optically spaced lettering can always be smaller.

Two kinds of spacing

At the same time I am not suggesting that the legibility of a direction sign can be exactly equated, as regards spacing, with reading matter; the eye has to travel over a much wider angle when reading a book, and this combined with considerable speed tends to make the judgement of spacing dependent more on peripheral vision than foveal vision.

Nevertheless, there is, I am sure, a more accurate form of spacing required when setting letters in a title page – whether in lower case or capitals. As soon as you stop to consider the precise position of a letter between two others you fixate the eye, and particularly the fovea, more than you do when reading text. For example, in the case of the capital 'L' between two 'I's the eye fixates on the three vertical strokes in turn and adjusts the centre vertical stroke (the 'L') more as if it were another 'I'. Peripheral vision, which surely must play a larger part in actual reading, is less demanding, and if this is a fact it should be taken into consideration.

An optical spacing instrument in use

My first great opportunity to demonstrate the possibilities of optical spacing came when Mr Brooke Crutchley, the University Printer at Cambridge, commissioned me to design an alphabet for use throughout the new building for the University Press. It is a fact that I did not dare tell the press that I was about to use my optical letter spacing instrument. However, all was well when the letters, 1 ft 10 in. high along the top of the building, were passed as satisfactory. Although I was fairly certain of letters 1 in. high, I had some doubts as to whether a simple enlargement together with a very large inter-letter constant would work.

For the doors etc. throughout the building we used Letraset with space guides (Figs. 33, 34, and 35).

PRESS REVISERS
MR CARDER
MR KIRKUP

Fig. 33

The sheets were arranged with markers that gave me the opportunity to expand or contract the spacing as you see in the top illustration of Fig. 34.

In the lower part of Fig. 34, you can see the method at work. The results of spacing this alphabet at three different sets can be seen in Fig. 35. First the wide, secondly at 'L' minimum fit, and thirdly close. Here you will notice how the letters begin to overlap, and the fourth set shows the letters stopped before this overlapping takes place.

The University Press, for whom it has been such a great pleasure to work and from whom I have, over many years, received such encouragement, did me no greater favour than having my alphabet made up into Letraset.

Fig. 34

ABCDEFGHIJKLM
NOPQRSTUVWXYZ
ABCDEFGHIJKLMN
OPQRSTUVWXYZ
ABCDEFGHIJKLMNOP
QRSTUVWXYZ
WAVE AVATA
ABCDEFGHIJKLMNOPQRSTUVWXYZ

Fig. 35

This soon led to an interest on the part of Letraset in my spacing technique and the following examples (Figs. 36, 37, 38, 39) are partly the result of their work and partly mine, but all of them are entirely in the experimental stage.

ABCDEFGHIJKLMN
OPQRSTUVWXYZ
MY THE QUICK FLED
BROWN GASP
MY THE QUICK BROWN
my the quick brown gal

Fig. 36

A WOMAN WHO KNOWS WHERE
SHE'S GOING CHOOSES CLOTHES
THAT LEND HER DISTINCTION

A Woman Who Knows Where
She's Going Chooses Clothes
That Lend Her Distinction

Fig. 37

**ABCDEFGHIJ
KLMNOPQRS
TUVWXYZ**

*ABCDEFGHIJ
KLMNOPQRS
TUVWXYZ*

ABCDEFGHIJ
KLMNOPQRS
TUVWXYZ

ABCDEFGHIJ
KLMNOPQRS
TUVWXYZ

Fig. 38

> It would seem therefore that when engravers working for book printers resorted to scribes for the patterns of their punches they were not obliged by technical reasons to do so On the other hand market and manuscript conditions would inevitably encourage the adoption of calligraphical models This however does not prove that printing is or was or ought to be based on calligraphy only that printing then as now was a business The copying of calligraphy is more difficult perhaps than the assimilation of inscriptional models but the calligraphical result achieved by such imitative means is artificial As a permanent method it should have been rejected because it is inconsistent with the nature of printing which is a department of engraving The imitation of calligraphy is excusable in the early period of printing because it was inevitable But while it is one thing to excuse the printers of the fifteenth century for deliberately copying hands familiar to their public it is impossible to be so indulgent towards the sixteenth century printers who reproduced the fashionable highly flourished German calligraphy

Fig. 39

Ten years later

With the gradual build-up of experience in the spacing of a greater variety of alphabets we have felt the need to look again at our light wedge and our graph. It seemed that alphabets constructed from fairly divergent stroke thickness needed a stronger force to comply with an eye-preferred centre. The errors would, of course, have been there in all alphabets, but of such a slight nature that the eye could not detect them.

On the other hand, we have become even more attracted to a second moment wedge – that is a wedge constructed on the square law. This you will remember is the law of inertia and, in spacing, that is what we are talking about. A letter has to reside between its neighbours in a 'still' position. If each letter in a word is in a 'still' position, then there is perfect spacing.

The word then stands with all its letters properly integrated and should therefore be more easily read as a whole.

Much experience was gained through remaining with a straight second moment wedge. Indeed, enough information was obtained to convince us that this progression was the right one. And yet there remained the need for some modification. The problem letter in some alphabets remained the same through all our work. Most letters have responded perfectly enough to our vertically straight second moment wedge but some 'C's have been unwilling to yield precisely to their eye-preferred centres.

The problem was how to retain the square law progression which we instinctively felt to be right and yet give more power to the terminals of a 'C'. The eye seems to scan the sides of letters to assess the centres in such a way as to suggest a stronger response from the serif and/or tail of some 'C's. Another more consistent but very minor error was that an 'O' always tended to have too large a space. If the 'C' centre was solved we felt the 'O' space would be too. However, the majority of 'C's did respond well.

Revised graph

The second problem derived from a misunderstanding of the characteristic rectangle spaces from which our graph is formed. It will be remembered (see Fig. 16) that it was assumed that the light transmitted through a letter centred over the wedge could be resolved in terms of space into a rectangle of letter height centred over the wedge and having the same transmitted light values. In fact this has proved only to be true where the type of alphabet is extremely 'bold'. This is unfortunate because it would have been easier to deal with one graph or one set of tables. The spacing of alphabets was fair for 'bold' to 'medium' weight letters but venturing on the 'light' kind of letter produced progressively inadequate spaces for wide letters.

The rectangles we now use for forming the graph are tailored to each alphabet in that the vertical and horizontal strokes are matched to the alphabet thus:

Fig. 40

As can be readily perceived these rectangles are very much nearer to the symbols of letters and could well become part of any alphabet. A small modification to the design of the machine has enabled us to measure the light and the width of an upright half of a rectangle – so the making of individual graphs for alphabets causes very little delay over the previous method that employed a universal graph.

Another point which is appropriate to bring in here is the inequality of spaces to the sides of letter strokes that are of equal weight. The fact that this is so should not dismay anyone. There is no law that these spaces should be equal, though most alphabets are rationalised in this way. The equal mathematical space dulls the whole texture of a page and in many cases gives 'I's so little room that the dense pattern of straight vertical strokes becomes dominant. Two 'O's should be very close but 'I's and other similar strokes must be further apart. Of course this is generally known, but not perhaps understood. We have made exhaustive tests by eye and the following diagram shows with Univers the kind of tendency generally to be found in all alphabets when hand spaced.

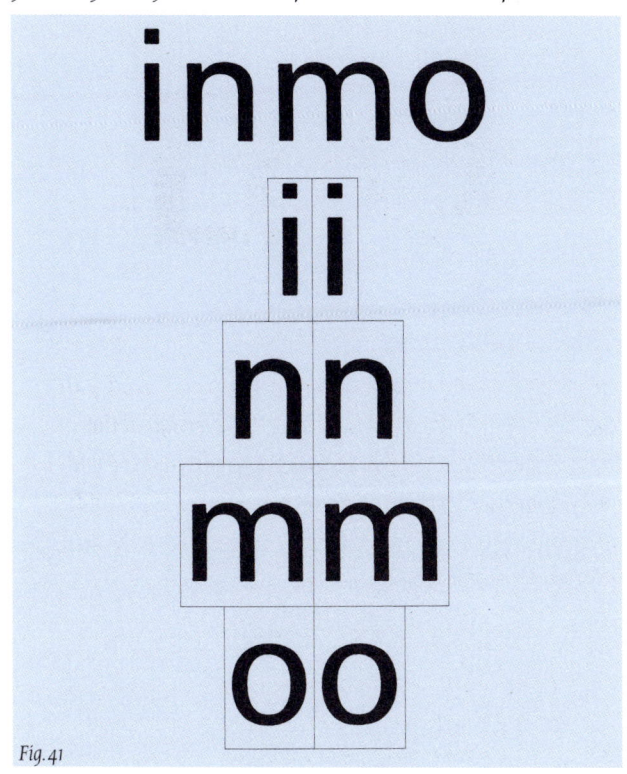

Fig. 41

Obviously the letter form with the largest internal space to stroke ratio needs least space outside of itself like the 'O'. Whereas a letter such as an 'I' needs all of its space externally. The human eye does not say – so to speak – here I see an upright stroke therefore give it such and such a space. The human eye sees the whole letter and requires a space outside that letter consistent with the dispersed black and white in the letter. This, of course, was done quite automatically in the case of scribes in the scriptoriums. The bolder and more condensed the letter form – take 'black' letter – the more consistent the spaces. The thinner or lighter the stroke and more extended the letter form the greater the variation of spaces.

The effect of paying attention to this natural optical characteristic is to give the page a remarkably consistent colour and at the same time avoid the 'picket fence' look of many type faces.

Computerised centres

One advantage of a computer is its speed. Speed means, to one searching for an answer to a problem, that many variants which are good guesses can be before you in no time at all. And this gives a more sure springboard for further action. Until recently all our experimental work involved the making of photographic wedges based on simple mathematical progressions, a process, nevertheless, that required a great deal of time. Sheer inertia prevented one from diversifying. Finally, having perfected the making of a straight second moment wedge, our ingenuity gave out. The introduction, for example, of a curved contour was beyond us and our equipment. First we asked the computer for verification of the results we obtained from our photographic wedge. They were perfect. We then tried the introduction of higher moments – really to get them out of the way because our intuition favoured the second moment so strongly. They did not show progress. We then tried expanding the second moment alternatively through the top and the bottom and this began to point to a solution. Soon we hope to have wedges made by computer but this takes a good deal of experimentation and therefore money – so it is not possible to show the results in displayed alphabets or text before going to print. However, here is a representation of the 'double parabola' wedge used for computing centres and spacing (Fig. 42), and overleaf are some of our test letters in computer print-out form (Fig. 43).

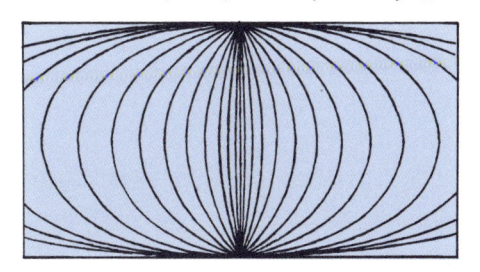

Fig. 42

Why my interest in the centres of letters? I have spoken of a letter being 'still' between its neighbours – not apparently pulled in one direction or another. To achieve this any one letter must align its own still centre with the vertical centre of its space. Find the formula for eye-preferred centres and one has found the formula for the space. To me this is self evident,

53

but it may not be to the reader. Imagine yourself as a letter 'I' standing upright with your hands by your side and legs together. Turn yourself into a 'T' and the centre of the forces remain as you were, equal on both sides, but the forces along the arms increase as the square law. Also the space you need increases in the same way. Supposing that you, as an 'A', meet a 'T'; the distance between you can be settled on the basis of the square law. Now turn yourself into an 'F', an asymmetrical shape. What happens now? The force along your arms will still increase according to the square law in such a way that your hands, small as they are compared to your body, have a force that compels you to lean away from the direction of your hands to keep the centre of forces in the same place, but because an 'F' is upright the

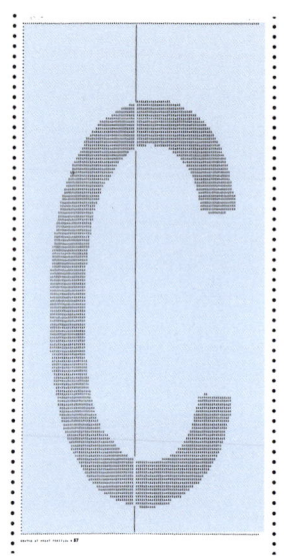

Fig. 43a

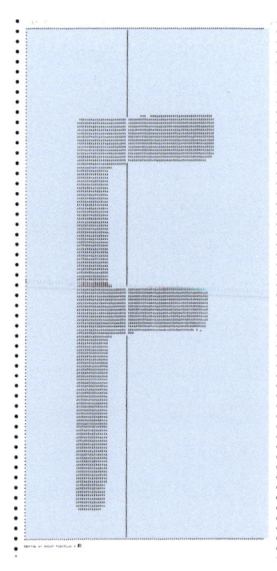

Fig. 43b

Fig. 43c

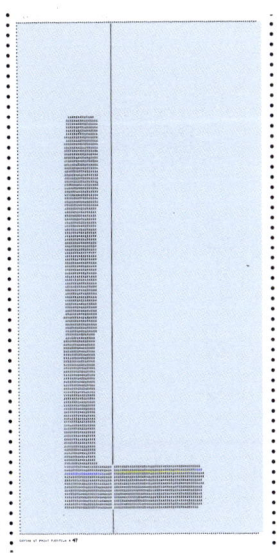

centre moves towards the hands. Now realise that what we experience with our own balance is also applied naturally enough to objects that we observe outside of ourselves. It is a commonplace that we see only what we know – hence perhaps the application of this square law to vision. If we space letters badly we notice it because we feel that it is not according to our experience. In spite of the object being weightless it is still given, by the eye, all the characteristics of a solid object. This may have been a tedious and altogether too simple an argument. However, I believe it to be one of the two most important ingredients of spacing. The other is to do with closeness. This to some extent under certain circumstances can modify the spacing. Art schools used to teach students that their compositions should either pass beyond the frame or be kept well within, but never finish just touching the frame. I think this is a valid statement. In the same way a letter should ideally override its neighbour if the square law dictates. However, there are purists who speak of letters as sacred. They say no letter should violate another by lapping over it. To meet this somewhat dreary concept, true spacing must at that point be abandoned. We are, of course, seeing more and more ligaturing of letters in display work and this is fun, but such an application to ordinary text would quickly render it illegible unless it were controlled by a system based on eye preferment. Fig. 44 shows what I would like to see – which is the top version of these two examples.

Fig. 44

Italics

What is the answer to the spacing of italics? Fig. 38 shows how far we had got in 1966. Progress has been very slow. The difficulty is that of deciding whether the wedge should be aligned with the slant of the particular italic alphabet being researched or whether the wedge should remain upright and out of alignment with the slant of the italic. The latter upright position seems the most logical. One does not tip one's head on one side to read italics. A further complication was the wedge itself. Our early wedges were not accurate enough for us to come to a definitive answer to this question. Sometimes we felt it should be one way and sometimes the other. However, since we have improved our technique and have lived with a very accurate second moment wedge which does give extremely good spacing results, we have become certain that the wedge should be tilted to the angle of the italic, as shown in Fig. 45.

Fig. 45

Sometimes I think I understand why the wedge has to be tilted. It must be accepted that if the centres of letters and spacing were only dependent on the impression falling on the retina, then an upright wedge would surely suffice. The fact that it seems to be otherwise might be that italics for our brain are upright letter forms slanted. Our brain for the purpose of spacing does not appear to differentiate between upright and slanting letters. It is as if the law of inertia is applied but without relation to gravity.

Finally, I would like to say that there has never been a moment like today where perfect spacing is a real possibility. Many photo-composing machines offer in their make-up the opportunity for this. Even if a unit system is used the units are very small and offer, in theory, a perfection of spacing equal or beyond that required by the eye. However, it is unlikely that this potential will be exploited as long as designers make their letters conform to unit widths rather than making the units fit the letters. I suppose the ideal situation would be to design an alphabet which spaced perfectly without kerning, but to obtain this result one certainly needs a computer programmed to assess the letters in terms of the square law.

Conclusion

There are many outlets for An Optical Letter Spacing Instrument. To name but a few:

1. The immediate assessment of a character thus achieving instant correctness of position within its right space. An entirely new symbol drawn and photographed in the previous few minutes could be incorporated correctly with the existing alphabet. Expansion and contraction of text by using a constant. If space assessment is incorrect to start with it will probably look worse if expanded.

2. It could be used for mechanical reading, as there is the ability to differentiate characters that have only small variations. Further, a very slight alteration in design can give a clearly differentiated signal. Thus it could help towards the demise of the alphabet developed for mechanical reading and with which the eye has such difficulty in coping.

3. In the design of alphabets for typewriters, wheels, etc., and other forms of printing that by their nature are limited to only a few unit spaces.

4. Traffic and directional signing. Applied letters.

THIS IS HOW IT ALL BEGAN

Bibliography

Sir Cyril Burt. A Psychological Study of Typography.
Stanley Morison. The Typographic Arts.
Richard Gregory. Eye and Brain.
Eric Gill. An Essay on Typography.
M. H. Pirenne. Vision and the Eye.
Sir D'Arcy Thompson. On Growth and Form.
P. H. Scholfield. The Theory of Proportion in Architecture.
David Kindersley. 'Towards perfect spacing' Book Design & Production, Vol. 5, No. 3, 1962
David Kindersley. 'Direction signs' Traffic Engineering and Control.
David Kindersley. Lecture to The Institute of Printing, Optical Letter Spacing
David Kindersley. Penrose Annual, Vol. 62, 1969.
Planned Seeing. H.M.S.O. Air Publication 3139 B.
R. L. Gregory. The Intelligent Eye.